Huntingdon Area
Middle School Library
Huntingdon, Pa.

THE WOLVES

BY JANA McCONOUGHEY

**EDITED BY
DR. HOWARD SCHROEDER**
Professor in Reading and Language Arts
Dept. of Elementary Education
Mankato State University

**PRODUCED AND DESIGNED BY
BAKER STREET PRODUCTIONS**
Mankato, MN

CRESTWOOD HOUSE
Mankato, Minnesota

LIBRARY OF CONGRESS CATALOGING IN PUBLICATION DATA

McConoughey, Jana
 The wolves

(Wildlife, habits and habitat)
SUMMARY: Discusses the habits and characteristics of wolves, once feared as vicious killers, but now understood to be gentle and peaceful wild animals, themselves in need of protection from hunters and encroaching civilization.
 1. Wolves--Juvenile literature. (1. Wolves) I. Schroeder, Howard. II. Title. III. Series.
QL737.C22M377   599.74'442   83-2086
ISBN 0-89686-225-9 (lib. bdg.)

International Standard Book Number:
Library Binding 0-89686-225-9

Library of Congress Catalog Card Number:
83-2086

ILLUSTRATION CREDITS:

Phil & Loretta Hermann: Cover
Lynn Rogers: 5, 9, 10, 13, 14, 18, 23, 24-25, 27, 28, 32, 35, 36, 38, 42-43, 45
Fish & Wildlife Service: 7
Bob Williams: 21
Rick Kolodziej: 41

Copyright© 1983 by Crestwood House, Inc. All rights reserved. No part of this book may be reproduced in any form without written permission from the publisher, except for brief passages included in a review. Printed in the United States of America.

Hwy. 66 South, Box 3427
Mankato, MN 56002-3427

TABLE OF CONTENTS

Introduction: 4
Chapter One: Portrait of the wolf 6
   What is a wolf?
   Wolves across North America
   A shy, clever animal
   An ideal home
Chapter Two: Hunting and Feeding 13
   A diet of meat
   Hunting in packs
   Making the kill
   Hunting alone
   Predator and prey on Isle Royale
   Wolves and livestock
Chapter Three: The wolf's society 23
   Leaders of the pack
   Wolves as communicators
   A pack and its territory
Chapter Four: Wolves and their families 31
   A close-knit family
   Preparing for the new pups
Chapter Five: Growth of the new pups 35
   Learning to become adults
   The first hunt
Chapter Six: Wolves and humans 40
   Wolves in zoos
   Hunting and Trapping
   Looking at wolves in a new way
Map: Wolf country 46
Glossary: 47

INTRODUCTION:

When the pilgrims came to America they found they were not alone. Bears, cougars, and wolves roamed among the trees. At night the settlers huddled in their homes, afraid to go outside. They were afraid of wild animals lurking about their cabins. They were most afraid of the wolves who howled constantly through the nights - wolves that killed and ate livestock, then left bloody bones for the terrified settlers to find. Stories of wolves attacking settlers spread from cabin to cabin. The wolf became the symbol of the feared, unknown wilderness.

There are still wolves in America today. There are not very many, though, and most people never see them except in zoos. Scientists now study wolves. They want to know more about this animal which frightened the early settlers. A few researchers have even made friends with wolves in the wild. They have lived close to them and studied them in their natural environment. These scientists say wolves are not mean and vicious. They say old stories of killer wolves were told out of fear and did not really happen. People today are beginning to believe these scientists.

However, wolves and people still do not live well

together. Wolves that live near farms sometimes invade the farmers' properties and eat their livestock. Like most wild animals, wolves simply eat what food they can find. Cattle and other farm animals are easy targets for them. But the killing of livestock is only one reason why wolves and people do not get along.

Many areas where wolves live are surrounded by farmlands. As people plant more crops, they cut down trees and plow under much of the land where wolves once lived. Wolves need trees or rocks to hide in, streams to drink from, and lots of room to run. They cannot live where people do. They are afraid of people and try to avoid them. For these reasons, wolves and people do not live well together.

A timber wolf roams the woods in northern Minnesota.

CHAPTER ONE:

What is a wolf?

The wolf is a wild dog. Almost all wolves in North America belong to a species called the gray wolf *(Canis lupus)*. It looks a lot like a German Shepherd, but is larger. Male wolves are usually two and a half to three feet tall (76-91 cm), and weigh seventy-five to one hundred pounds (36-50 kg). The largest wolf ever found weighed 175 pounds (79 kg), but wolves this large are rare. Females are smaller. They are usually one and a half to two and a half feet tall (46-76 cm) and weigh sixty to eighty pounds (30-40 kg). Generally, the farther north you go, the larger the wolves are. Wolves in Canada and Alaska are larger than wolves in the southern United States and Mexico. Wolves look much like the coyotes, but are much larger.

Wolves are found in many colors. Their color depends on their environment. They can be different shades of gray, brown, golden brown, rusty red, or almost any combination of these colors. Some are pure white and others are all black. The belly and throat is usually lighter and almost white. The nose, ears and legs are often light brown. The back and face are generally marked with dark brown or black.

The small red wolf is found in Texas and Louisiana.

Gray is the most common color of the wolf. The wolves of central Canada are usually gray. Wolves that live on the tundras or in the forests of Canada and Alaska may also be gray. Because of this, the nickname "gray wolf" is given by scientists to all wolves of North America. Even the red wolf, which is a small, red, fox-like wolf, is said to be a type of gray wolf.

In pioneer days wolves could be found in almost

every part of North America. There are still many wolves in Canada and Alaska. However, only about a thousand wolves remain in the lower forty-eight states of the United States. Only a few hundred wolves remain in Mexico.

Wolves across North America

The wolf has acquired many nicknames throughout North America, depending upon its habitat or color.

There are many wolves that live in the forests of Alaska, Canada, upper Michigan, northern Minnesota and northern Wisconsin. These wolves are called timber wolves because they live among the trees. Most timber wolves are dark gray. A few of them are black. Their home in the forest is dark and shadowy. This makes their dark coats a perfect camouflage.

Wolves that live in northern Alaska and Canada are called tundra wolves. They live on the treeless plains, or tundras, of extreme North America. Tundra wolves are the most beautiful wolves found in North America. Their fur is very thick to protect them from the cold. Some of these wolves are pure white so that they can easily hide in their snowy environment.

A few wolves live in Arizona, Arkansas, Mississippi, Missouri, New Mexico, and North Dakota. These wolves are smaller than the wolves of the far North. White, black and brown hairs mix to make these wolves look gray. This small gray wolf also lives in Mexico.

The red wolf lives in small parts of Texas and Louisiana. It is nearly extinct.

A black timber wolf.

A timber wolf soaks up some sun on a cool, spring day.

A shy, clever animal

Wolves are very shy animals. They do not like to fight and only do so when they have no other choice. Wolves are normally gentle animals. They are very caring and loving with other wolves.

There are times when a wolf may be injured or killed by a large animal, like a moose, that it attacks for food. However, the only natural enemies the wolf has are humans and sometimes bears.

Wolves avoid humans whenever possible. If a wolf smells a human nearby, it will run away or hide. Scientists say wolves are afraid of humans. Even when people threaten a wolf's home or babies, the wolf will keep its distance. Scientists have carefully taken baby wolves away from their parents so they can study them. The mother and father wolves did not attack the scientists. They just barked!

Wolves are also very intelligent animals. They are smarter than any pet dog. A wolf can learn to fetch a stick or roll over much faster than a dog. Because they live in the wild, wolves must always be very alert. Their alertness helps them to learn many things from their environment.

Wolves can also be very clever at times. In one instance, when a scientist approached a wolf den to count the pups, the father of the pups ran off. The mother stood aside and barked at the intruder. The scientist counted and measured the pups. Then he stood and turned to leave. He was surprised to find the father of the pups sitting several feet behind him, watching his every move!

An ideal home

Almost any environment can be home to a wolf. The two places where wolves cannot live are the desserts of the western United States, and the dense, wet forests of southeastern Mexico. The wolf is a playful animal and likes to romp through trees and rocks. A favorite environment is one with hills and flatlands cut by ravines and canyons. A wolf likes to have a river or stream nearby where it can stretch out on the bank and enjoy the sun. What a wolf **must** have in its environment is a place to escape from its enemies. The wolf prefers a wooded area where it can hide. The wolf that does not live in a wooded area, like the tundra wolf, must rely on speed to help it escape. This wolf, then, needs large, open plains where it can outrun its enemies.

CHAPTER TWO:

A diet of meat

Wolves are large, energetic animals and need a lot of food. They are carnivores, which means they eat mostly meat. A healthy adult wolf can eat twenty pounds (9 kg) of meat at one feeding. That would be about eighty hamburgers for a human!

The wolf uses its large teeth to catch and eat other animals.

Wolves eat very large animals or many small animals, depending on what is available. They prefer to eat larger animals. Ungulates, or hoofed animals, such as moose, deer, caribou, musk-oxen, and elk make up much of the diet of most wolves. Red wolves, however, are an exception to this. These wolves live in areas of Texas where there are few of these hoofed animals. They resort to eating the smaller animals that are most abundant, such as rabbits, beavers, and mice. They will even eat frogs and insects on occasion. This type of diet is fine for the red wolf, which is the smallest member of the wolf family.

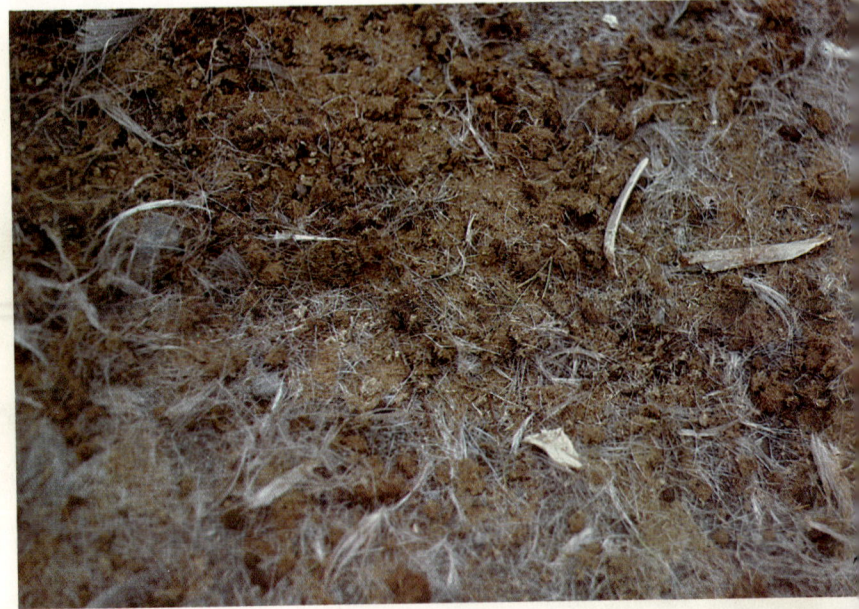

This is all that's left after a wolf pack killed and ate a whitetail deer.

Hunting in packs

The wolf is a powerful runner. It can run for long distances, but not at very high speeds. Although the wolf can outrun people, it has trouble overtaking hoofed animals. Wolves often solve this problem by hunting in groups called "packs." Hunting in packs allows the wolves to form a circle around their prey. The prey is caught in the middle, and cannot run from the wolves.

The main purpose of forming a pack is to make it easier for the wolves to hunt large, hoofed animals. However, wolves within a pack have been seen to eat small animals, too.

A wolf pack may have from three to twenty members. More than twenty in a pack is unusual. Once a pack gets any larger, it is hard to catch enough food for everyone.

Hoofed animals, such as caribou, are migratory animals. This means they constantly roam from area to area. The pack may have to travel many miles in a single day or night before it finds a herd of caribou to prey upon. It is easy, though, for a wolf to cover such a distance. Wolves always travel at a steady trot and rarely walk. They can travel forty miles without rest.

Wolves track down herds of prey with their keen sense of smell. As the pack gets closer to the herd, the smell of the prey gets stronger. They stay back, though, and do not rush in at the herd. Instead, they approach their prey very slowly. They creep forward and cautiously study the herd.

The wolves look for an animal that is old, sick, or very young. These animals cannot run as fast as the others in the herd. The pack knows that a strong, healthy deer or caribou is probably too quick for them. A healthy animal that can defend itself, or can outrun the wolves, is rarely attacked. Scientists say they have seen a healthy moose charge a pack of hungry wolves. The wolves turned and fled!

Wolves actually help keep herds of deer, musk-oxen and other animals healthy. Killing the old or sick members of the herd leaves more food for the remaining animals. With more food, the healthy animals are able to have strong, healthy young.

Making the kill

Once a wolf pack has decided which member of the herd to kill, it begins its stalk. The wolves situate themselves around the prey. They are still far enough away that the prey cannot see them. Next, they sneak as close to the prey as they can. If they are careful, the wolves can get to within thirty feet (9 m) of their prey without being noticed.

The pack continues to stalk closer until they are seen by their prey. Then they stop and stand very still. Usually neither wolves nor prey move for several minutes. They just stand and stare at each other. Wolves almost never attack their prey while it is standing still; they wait until the animal tries to run. When the prey finally makes a move, the wolves react by rushing at it from all sides. Scientists think that this is just a natural response — when the prey moves, instinct causes the wolves to attack. Though the prey may flee for several yards, it rarely escapes. The wolves grab it with their powerful jaws and pull it to the ground.

Though wolves are clever when it comes to hunting, they are not always successful. Sometimes the prey spots the wolves before they have stalked close enough to rush it. If the prey runs off, the pack may chase it for a few yards but soon gives up. They know their only chance for catching an animal like a deer or an elk is by surrounding it and rushing it from a short distance. When chasing large prey, such as moose, they are able to make a kill only ten to twenty percent of the time. For this reason wolves are very careful when they hunt.

When the pack has made a kill and eaten the meat, the wolves wander off to a sunny place and rest. The meat in their stomachs digests quickly as they sleep. After several hours of lounging around, the wolves

This pack was able to kill a whitetail deer.

are ready to return to their kill. After eating any meat that is left, they spend hours chewing on the bones. This keeps their teeth clean and strong, and supplies them with minerals. By the time the wolves are finished with their kill, only fur and a few bones remain.

Hunting alone

Wolves in a pack are normally very friendly to each other. However, when a pack becomes too large, some of the younger wolves must be forced to leave. These wolves become loners and hunt alone until they are accepted into a new pack. Lone wolves are unable to catch larger animals by themselves. They usually stalk squirrels, rabbits and beavers. Because wolves prefer bigger game, loners try to join a pack if they can find one. Occasionally, several lone wolves will find each other and join to form an entirely new pack.

Predator and prey on Isle Royale

Today scientists are studying the relationship between wolves and their prey. Scientists are especially interested in the wolves of Isle Royale, an island in northern Lake Superior. The wolves of Isle Royale prey mainly upon moose. Large numbers of moose and wolves have been living on the island for many years. In recent years, however, the number of moose on the island has fallen sharply.

Isle Royale is a perfect place for scientists to conduct a study on moose and wolf populations. Because it is an island, the moose and wolves cannot leave. This fact makes the scientists' job much easier. It leaves no doubt that the number of moose is declining because more moose are dying; not because the animals are leaving the area. It also means that new wolves cannot come into the area unless they are born there. Scientists don't think there are any more wolves on the island than usual, and they are probably not eating any more moose than they used to.

Scientists think that recent harsh winters on the island may have caused the decline in moose. They think that the thick snows may have made it hard for even the healthy, young moose to escape the wolves.

As a result, the wolves may have eaten fewer old and sick moose, and more healthy moose that are at the reproductive age (those old enough to have calves). This means that fewer moose would be born the following spring.

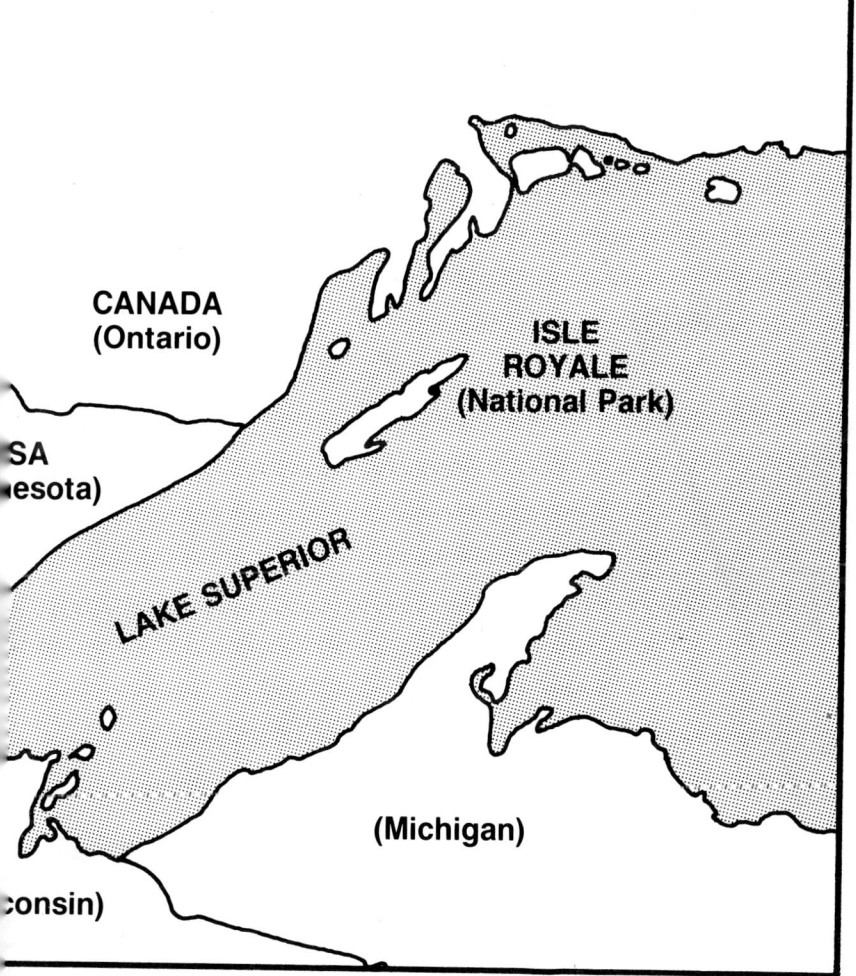

Isle Royale is an island in Lake Superior, located south of Ontario and east of Minnesota.

Scientists must find out why the moose number is declining if they are to save the moose population. If the moose die out, many of the island's wolves will starve. Scientists do not want this to happen to these animals and are continuing their studies.

Wolves and livestock

Wolves do not normally eat livestock or domestic animals. They will, however, if they are very hungry or cannot find any wild game. Expanding human population has driven away the herds of elk, deer and other animals that wolves prey upon. As a result, wolves sometimes come onto farmsteads and eat cattle.

In the United States and Canada angry farmers have sometimes poisoned wolves to keep them from killing livestock. Scientists and conservationists are looking for a way to prevent this poisoning. One way is to move the wolves to areas where there is no livestock for them to kill.

Conservation officials have taken wolves living near farms and moved them to wooded areas. The wolves are moved to wilderness areas in which there are already wolves living. The transported wolves adapt easily to their new homes.

CHAPTER THREE:

Because most wolves hunt in packs, they must get along well with each other. Whether or not a hunt is successful depends on how well the wolves can work together. If the wolves of a pack were to constantly fight, they would injure each other. A pack full of injured wolves would not be able to catch their prey. So, to keep peace among themselves, wolves follow a strict social order. Each member of the pack has a rank, just like a private or captain in the army.

The "alpha male" is the leader of the wolf pack.

Leaders of the pack

The leader of the pack is always a male. Scientists call him the "alpha male." It is the alpha male that

The alpha male has decided that this pack will go on a hunt.

decides when the pack will go on a hunt, and when and where the pack can rest. All other wolves in the pack respect him. If the alpha male wanders from the pack for a short time, the other wolves fondly greet him when he returns. They gather around him and gently nuzzle him and lick his face. When the pack

makes a kill, the wolves wait and let the alpha male have first choice at the meat. Once he has decided which part of the prey he wants and has started eating, the others begin to feed. When a pack is ready to rest after feeding on the kill, they all follow the leader to the resting spot of his choice. The alpha male may change his mind and move to a new spot after an hour of resting. Then all the other wolves get up and move with him. When he is done resting and ready to move on, he walks up to each of the other wolves and wakes them. Then he rounds them up and the pack moves on.

There is also an "alpha female" in the pack. She and the alpha male are almost always mates. The alpha female is dominant over all other females in the pack, and also over many of the males. She sometimes helps the male keep the other wolves in line. The male is usually dominant; but when they mate and have pups, the female becomes the boss!

Besides the alpha wolves, the other wolves with a definite rank are the "peripheral wolves." These are usually adult wolves that were once loners and are now trying to join the pack. They are called peripheral wolves because they do not get involved with the higher ranked members of the pack. Peripheral wolves may also be smaller and weaker wolves that shy away from the larger wolves. They are ranked at the bottom of the pack.

Between the alpha wolves and the peripheral

Some "peripheral wolves" are lone wolves that are trying to join the pack.

wolves are the rest of the adult wolves in the pack. They are ranked among themselves from highest to lowest. If two of these wolves ever disagree on anything, the higher ranked wolf always gets his way. In this way, wolves in the pack avoid actual fighting and injury. Wolves do not usually have a rank until they are at least two years old.

Wolves as communicators

Wolves are very good communicators. They use sounds and gestures to show their rank or dominance. A wolf will show its rank by baring its teeth and growling. If another wolf comes closer and growls back, it means it is not afraid and is of an even higher rank. If it rolls over on its back and whimpers, it means the wolf is of a lower rank. Usually the larger of the two wolves will be the higher ranked. Rolling over on its back is the smaller wolf's way of showing that it respects the first wolf. This rolling-over action is seen many times in domestic dogs as well. Dogs often roll over on their backs when their

A wolf snarls to threaten other members of the pack.

masters approach, to show their respect.

Wolves must communicate other things besides rank. They can make a variety of sounds. Each sound has its own meaning. If a wolf whimpers, it means he is restless or excited. Wolves also whimper when they bring food to their pups. This is how they draw the pups' attention. A snarl means that a wolf is threatening another wolf. For example, if a father wolf plays too rough with his pups, the mother wolf will snarl at him. It is her way of telling the father to "take it easy."

A short **wuff** is a warning sound. When a member of the pack senses danger, he alerts other pack members by making this sound. If the danger becomes stronger, the **wuff** turns into a bark. Pack members know it is time to flee when they hear a bark.

The sound that wolves are famous for, however, is their howl. When you hear a group of wolves howl, it is easy to understand why the early settlers were so afraid. Usually one wolf starts howling and soon the whole pack joins in. If two wolves of the pack are howling on the same note, one will quickly change. The different sounds together make an eerie noise. If there are any other wolf packs in the area, they will also join in the chorus. In pioneer days, when wolves were found everywhere, the nights were filled with howls from every direction. The settlers must have felt surrounded!

Scientists do not know for sure why wolves howl. Some say lone wolves howl because they are lonely and are trying to find other wolves. However, most scientists agree that wolf packs probably howl because they are staking out their territory and telling other packs to stay away.

A pack and its territory

Each wolf pack has its own territory which it defends from other packs. Territories may stretch for fifty to sixty miles (80-90 km), or they may only be a few square miles. It is important to wolves that they have their own territory. If the pack has to leave its territory to find food, it always returns after the hunt. Without a home territory to raise them in, wolves in a pack will not even mate or have pups. If there is abundant prey for the pack to feed on in its territory, it will stay there for many years. More often, though, the amount of food available to the wolves varies and a pack may have several territories over the years. Once a pack is settled in a territory, its wolves can begin raising their families.

CHAPTER FOUR:

Wolf family members always show a great deal of love and affection for each other. A wolf's family is a lot like a human's family. Wolves are usually mates for life. Young wolves stay with their parents until they are at least several years old.

A close-knit family

Wolves mate only once a year in the late winter months. Females are able to become pregnant for only a few days during that time. Males stay very close to their mates and become jealous and snarl at any other males that come near.

A female wolf is very careful about who her mate is. Several of the younger males in the pack will try to become her mate. During her first mating season, a young female will choose a male that will be her mate for life. If one of the newly formed couple should die, the other one usually will never mate again.

The amount of mating is controlled by the alpha female. If the pack gets too large, maybe only she will mate. This controls the size of the pack.

The "alpha female" controls the amount of mating in a pack.

Preparing for the new pups

After the mating process occurs, it will be sixty to sixty-two days until the pups are born. The pregnant female begins digging a den in the ground three to four weeks before her pups arrive. Her mate, and even other members of the pack, may help her. She often searches several days for the right spot to dig the den. It must be built on high ground so that water does not seep into it. It must also be built near a river or stream. This is important because once the female starts nursing her young, she will need to drink a lot of water.

Wolf dens are quite large. The front entrance is usually large enough for a grown man to crawl through. A tunnel, which is sometimes even larger, leads from the front opening to the chamber where the pups are kept. The tunnel may be from six to fourteen feet (2-4 m) long. The chamber is tall enough for the mother wolf to stand in. The floor of the chamber is dirt. Some wolf dens may have two chambers. The pups are kept in one and the mother sometimes rests in the other. There may also be more than one entrance.

Once the dens are dug, it will not be long before the pups are born. While waiting, the entire pack stays close to the dens. They hunt for food close by, instead of going on long hunts.

The female stays very close to the den until the pups are born. She eats small animals that she can catch nearby. She licks the floor of the den many times to clean it. The day before the pups are born, she goes inside and stays until the pups arrive. Her mate stays outside, close to the entrance.

Usually there are four to seven pups in a litter. They are born ten to sixty minutes apart. When the first pup is born, the female cleans it at once. There is a thin, clear film covering the pup called an amniotic sac. She breaks this sac with her tongue and removes it by licking the pup. Next she chews through the umbilical cord. This is a cord which is attached to the pup's stomach at one end and to the placenta inside the mother at the other end. Food passes through the umbilical cord from the placenta to the pup's stomach until it is born.

Once the mother has chewed through the umbilical cord, she licks the pup again until it is very clean. Finally, she eats the amniotic sac and the umbilical cord. This keeps the den clean and provides her with good nourishment. Then the mother curls protectively around her pup and rests until the next one is born. After the last pup is born, the placenta leaves her body. She eats this also. Then she licks the floor of the den until there is no trace of the birth of the pups.

CHAPTER FIVE:

Baby wolves are born deaf and with their eyes closed, just like domestic pups. They all have dark brown or gray fur and large round heads with pug noses. Each one weighs about one pound (0.5 kg) at birth. For the first ten or twelve days of their lives they do nothing but sleep and nurse. The mother leaves the den only to drink. Her mate brings food to her.

After about twelve days, the pups are able to open their eyes. Once they can see, they begin to investigate the den. They learn to stand and then to walk. Their front teeth come in about this time and they begin chewing gently on each other's tails. By the time they are three weeks old, they can hear and see very well. It is time now for them to go outside and investigate.

The pups come out of their den.

The other pack members become very excited when they see the pups for the first time. They gather around, wagging their tails and licking them. This is usually the first time the father is able to get close to his pups. He stands guard over them while the other pack members continue to greet them.

All of the wolves are very protective of the pups in the pack. During the next few months the pups will spend a lot of time playing outside. Many pack

New pups spend much of their time sleeping.

members will take turns standing guard over them. If the pups' mother must leave for food or water, another wolf will rush over to "babysit." If something should happen to the mother of the pups and she should die, the other wolves quickly move the pups to the den of another female. They will be raised by that female as if they were her own.

When the pups are about four weeks old, they begin to eat solid food. When an adult wolf returns from eating a meal, the pups swarm around and nuzzle it. The adult wolf then spits up part of its dinner. The pups quickly devour it. All members of the pack help feed the pups in this way. The pups can nuzzle any wolf in the pack and it will feed them. After the pups are six to eight weeks old, their mother begins to nip at them whenever they try to nurse from her. This is her way of telling her pups that they are too old to nurse. By the time they are eight weeks old, they eat only solid food.

Learning to become adults

At three months of age, the pups begin to learn the ways of the adult wolves. The mother no longer allows the pups to sleep in the den. She growls at them and chases them away if they try to enter. The

After the pups are three months old, they no longer sleep in the den.

pups begin to sleep outside with the rest of the wolves.

All of the pups in the pack begin sleeping outside at about the same time, since the litters of a pack are normally born within a few days of each other. When the pups begin sleeping outside, the other wolves of the pack begin to go on longer hunting trips again. Several of the younger adult wolves of the pack stay behind with the pups. They feed them and take care of them. After several days, the pack returns. Some of the wolves carry pieces of raw meat and bones in their mouths to give to the pups. In this way, the pups learn what fresh meat tastes like.

The first hunt

Once the pups have eaten fresh meat, they are ready to learn how to catch it. The young adult wolves become more than just babysitters now. They are the ones who teach the pups how to hunt. While the older wolves are out on their hunting expedition, the pups go out with their teachers on a hunt of their own. The young adult wolves show them how to track down their prey. They teach the pups how to stalk it and then how to attack it. From this point on, the pups will hunt their own food.

When winter sets in, the baby wolves are really no longer babies. They are almost as big as the adult wolves. By this time, they are hunting with the rest of the pack. It will be another year and a half before they are totally grown, though. Wolves do not reach physical maturity until they are two years old. At that time they may decide to leave and start their own pack. If they stay, they will become teachers for the next generation of pups.

CHAPTER SIX:

It may seem that a wolf would make a good pet. This is not true. The wolf is a wild animal and should be left where it belongs; in freedom. They need trees or rocks where they can hide. They also need hills of dirt where they can build their dens. Wolves are energetic animals. They need lots of room. And, of course, they need plenty of food and water.

Wolves in zoos

Many zoos in North America have wolves. Some of the zoos, usually the smaller ones, keep wolves in cages that are too small. Visitors at the zoo are allowed too close to the cages. In these small cages the wolves have nowhere to go to avoid the visitors. It makes them very nervous. That is the reason you often see caged wolves pacing back and forth. It is against their natural instincts to stay so close to humans. When people see the wolves pacing back and forth, they think that the wolves are mean and vicious. They should understand that the wolves are acting differently than they would if they were in the wild.

There are some zoos in North America that have very good habitat for wolves. They have large fenced in areas with hills, rocks and trees inside. The pens are large enough so that the wolves can run around instead of just pace back and forth. And there is plenty of space between the wolves and the visitors. The wolves in these pens are not nervous and afraid. They even wag their tails and greet the zoo keeper at feeding time. People who see wolves in these zoos understand how friendly and gentle wolves really are.

Good zoos have large pens with natural habitat.

A timber wolf at sunset.

Hunting and trapping

Though it is illegal in most of the United States to kill a wolf, it is not illegal to kill them in Alaska. There are so many wolves left in Alaska that scientists are not real worried about their becoming extinct. The same is true in Canada. In fact, many wolves are hunted in these areas. They may be shot or trapped for their fur. A wolf hunter or trapper can earn more than $150 by selling the fur of just one wolf. Wolf hunting and trapping is not as popular in all areas of North America as it used to be.

In areas of North America where hunting and trapping are legal, these activities are carefully regulated. Government officials carefully limit hunting and trapping of wolves so that the animals don't become scarce.

In 1973, the United States passed the Endangered Species Act. This act prohibits the killing of timber wolves anywhere in the United States, except Alaska.

Looking at wolves in a new way

Only in recent years have people accepted wolves for what they really are. When the settlers came to America, they already were afraid of wolves. Myths and legends about evil wolves had been passed down to them by their ancestors. Fortunately, we are beginning to see wolves in a different way. Wolves are interesting and beautiful animals. It would be sad if they became a thing of the past.

MAP:

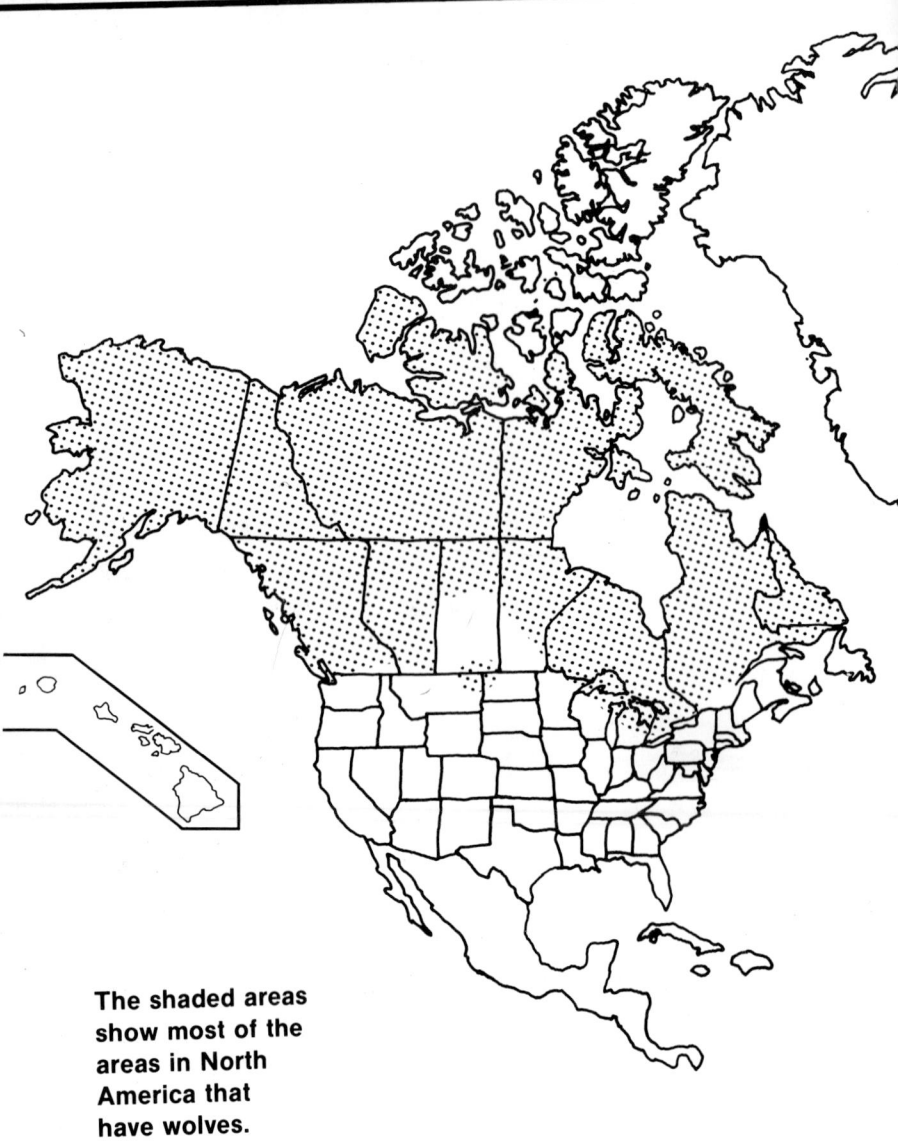

The shaded areas show most of the areas in North America that have wolves.

GLOSSARY:

AMNIOTIC SAC - A thin sac that surrounds the baby animal when it is born.

CARNIVORE - An animal that eats mainly meat.

CAMOUFLAGE - Coloring that keeps something from being easily seen and recognized.

ENVIRONMENT - The natural surroundings of an animal; its neighborhood.

KILL SITE - The place where an animal, or animals, kill and eat their prey.

LONER WOLF - A wolf without a pack to belong to.

MIGRATORY - Animals that continue to move from one place to another.

PLACENTA - An organ inside the mother animal that feeds the baby; food and nourishment pass from the placenta through the umbilical cord to the baby before birth.

PREY - An animal taken by a predator as food.

SOCIAL ORDER - Each member in a society has a specific rank.

SPECIES - A group of animals that look and act alike.

STALK - To pursue prey carefully or slowly.

UMBILICAL CORD - A cord that connects a baby to its mother and passes food and wastes between them before birth.

UNGULATES - Any animal that has hoofs.

WILDLIFE
HABITS & HABITAT

READ AND ENJOY THE SERIES:

THE **WHITETAIL**

THE **BALD EAGLE**

THE **WOLVES**

THE **PHEASANT**

THE **BEAVER**

THE **MALLARD**

THE **FOXES**

THE **SQUIRRELS**